Earth's Changing
Deserts

by Neil Morris

Raintree

www.raintreepublishers.co.uk

Visit our website to find out more information about **Raintree** books.

To order:

 Phone 44 (0) 1865 888112

 Send a fax to 44 (0) 1865 314091

📭 Visit the Raintree Bookshop at **www.raintreepublishers.co.uk** to browse our catalogue and order online.

First published in Great Britain by Raintree, Halley Court, Jordan Hill, Oxford OX2 8EJ, part of Harcourt Education.
Raintree is a registered trademark of Harcourt Education Ltd.

Editorial: Nick Hunter and Catherine Clarke
Design: Michelle Lisseter and Bridge Creative Services Ltd
Picture Research: Maria Joannou and Liz Eddison
Illustrations: Bridge Creative Services Ltd
Production: Jonathan Smith

Originated by Dot Gradations Ltd
Printed and bound in China by South China Printing Company

ISBN 1 844 21394 3
07 06 05 04 03
10 9 8 7 6 5 4 3 2 1

British Library Cataloguing in Publication Data
Morris, Neil
Earth's Changing Deserts. – (Landscapes and People)
551.4'15
A full catalogue record for this book is available from the British Library.

Acknowledgements
The publishers would like to thank the following for permission to reproduce photographs: Bruce Coleman Collection pp. 4 (P. Kaya), **11** (Natural Selection Inc.), **14** (Granville Harris); Corbis pp. **19** (Penny Tweedie), **20** (Robert van der Hilst), **21** (Buddy Mays), **22**, **28** (Carl & Ann Purcell); Getty Images (Stone) p. **27**; NHPA pp. **7** (Anthony Bannister), **13** (Daniel Heuclin), **17** (Daniel Heuclin), **23** (Kevin Schafer), **25** (Nigel J. Dennis); Oxford Scientific Films pp. **10** (Richard Packwood), **15** (Deni Brown), **16** (Eyal Bartov), **29** (Doug Allan); Still Pictures (Jorgen Schytte) **26**.

Cover photograph of a camel caravan in the Takla Makan Desert reproduced with permission of Corbis (Keren Su).

The publishers would like to thank Margaret Mackintosh for her assistance in the preparation of this book.

Every effort has been made to contact copyright holders of any material reproduced in this book. Any omissions will be rectified in subsequent printings if notice is given to the publishers.

Contents

Any words appearing in the text in bold, **like this**, are explained in the Glossary.

What is a desert?

What do you think of when you think of a desert? Is it a very hot place, with **sand dunes** as far as the eye can see? Or is it a flat wilderness, where the dry ground is covered in rocks and stones? Whichever one you think of, you're right. A desert can be both of these things, and others too.

A desert is an area of very dry land. It is dry because very little rain falls in that particular region. In fact, deserts receive less than 25 centimetres of rain in a whole year. This means that the ground is dry nearly all the time. Most places in the world have much more rainfall. London, for example, receives about 60 centimetres of rain every year. New York, USA, has about 110 centimetres, and Sydney, Australia, has about 120 centimetres of rain each year.

∩ *These huge sand dunes dwarf a four-wheel-drive vehicle as it crosses the Sahara Desert in Algeria.*

The biggest desert in the world, the Sahara in Africa, is very hot. The daytime summer temperature is usually around 32° Celsius. There are different desert **landscapes**, though. Some deserts, such as the Gobi Desert in Asia, are much cooler for most of the year. The summer temperature in the Gobi Desert is about 21° Celsius, but in winter the daytime temperature drops to −12° Celsius.

The icy **polar** regions of Earth are desert regions, too, and the temperatures there are very low. In Antarctica, where the ground is frozen for most of the year, the summer temperature varies between −15° Celsius and −35° Celsius.

World of deserts

There are big deserts on six **continents** of the world – Africa, Antarctica, Asia, Oceania, North America and South America. Smaller areas of very dry land are also found on the seventh continent, Europe, especially in southern Spain.

Looking at deserts

Earth's deserts formed and spread over millions of years. Since then, they have been constantly changing. They are home to many different kinds of plants and animals that have **adapted** to a tough life with little water. People, too, have tried to control the deserts for living and farming, and we continue to change them.

> *Hot deserts are found in two bands that stretch around the world. The bands are near the **tropics**, which is Earth's hottest region. Cooler deserts are further from the **equator**. The coldest desert is on the frozen continent of Antarctica.*

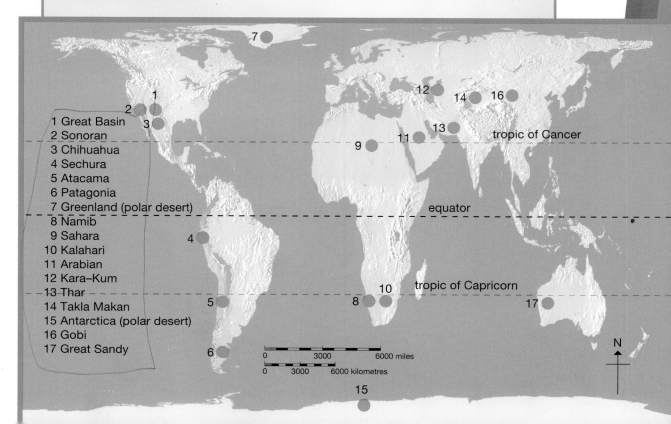

1 Great Basin
2 Sonoran
3 Chihuahua
4 Sechura
5 Atacama
6 Patagonia
7 Greenland (polar desert)
8 Namib
9 Sahara
10 Kalahari
11 Arabian
12 Kara–Kum
13 Thar
14 Takla Makan
15 Antarctica (polar desert)
16 Gobi
17 Great Sandy

tropic of Cancer

equator

tropic of Capricorn

0   3000   6000 miles
0   3000   6000 kilometres

N

How are deserts formed?

Water changes in the air, making clouds and then rain. First the Sun heats water on land and in the oceans. The heated water then changes into a gas called water vapour, which rises into the air. As the vapour cools it forms droplets of water, which join together to form clouds. Eventually the water falls back to Earth as rain, snow, sleet or hail. These are all different forms of **precipitation**.

Deserts are formed by a lack of precipitation. There are various reasons why a particular region should have little rainfall and so be very dry. Most hot deserts are found in the **tropical** regions just to the north and south of the **equator**. As masses of air move towards the equator, they heat up and rise high into the sky. Then the air cools, forms clouds and drops rain over regions where tropical **rainforests** grow. By the time masses of air reach the lines of the **tropics** (see page 5), they are dry again. The air drops down, and dry winds blow across the regions where deserts are found. There the skies are cloudless and clear, so the Sun heats up the ground very quickly. The masses of air are huge and constantly moving.

◠ *The trade winds push air towards the equator, where it heats up, rises and moves towards the tropics. Many deserts are near the **latitudes** of the tropics.*

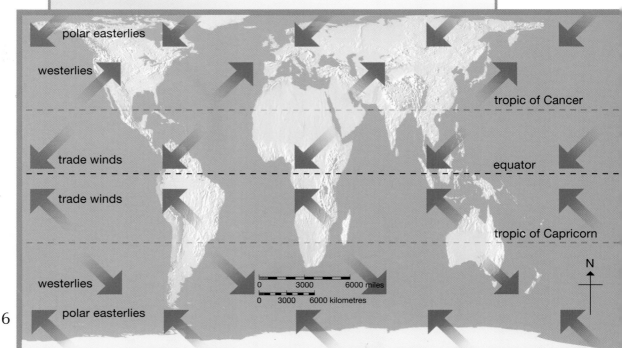

polar easterlies

westerlies

tropic of Cancer

trade winds

equator

trade winds

tropic of Capricorn

N

westerlies

0   3000   6000 miles
0   3000   6000 kilometres

polar easterlies

∩ *Mist rolling in from the Atlantic Ocean covers this coastal region of the Namib Desert in southern Africa.*

Far from the sea

Other areas become deserts because they are so far from the sea. The winds that blow inland from the ocean have dropped their rain by the time they reach the middle of a **continent**, or large land mass. The Gobi Desert is in the middle of Asia: it is so far inland that the winds have lost all their **moisture** before they get there.

Along the coast

Some deserts, such as the Atacama in South America, form along the coast. In these regions the seas have cold **currents**, which means the air does not take up much moisture and the winds blowing off the seas are cool and dry. This helps to cause desert. Mist often forms over these coastal deserts, but the ground remains dry. Summer temperatures are generally around 18° Celsius in the Atacama Desert.

In the rain shadow

Some areas become deserts because they are on the sheltered side of high mountains. As clouds rise to pass over the mountains, they cool down and drop rain on the slopes below. When the winds reach the other side, they have lost their moisture and are dry.

At night

Deserts are cold places at night. This is because there is no cloud cover. In wetter regions, clouds act like a blanket and keep in the warmth at night. In the desert, though, the temperature may drop by 30° Celsius when the Sun goes down.

Changing landscapes

There are many different desert **landscapes**. Some deserts are rocky, others are stony, and some of the most famous deserts are sandy. These sandy deserts are also called **ergs** (from an Arabic word for 'area of sand') – but where does the sand come from? It comes from rocks, and it forms over millions of years. As rocks are heated rapidly by the Sun during the day, they expand (or get bigger). Then as they cool quickly at night, the rocks contract (get smaller). This causes them to crack. Gradually the rocks begin to crumble into smaller stones and then eventually into tiny grains of sand.

The Arabian Desert covers parts of nine countries and has three main regions. The Syrian Desert is mainly made up of a stony plain. The An Nafud and Rub' al Khali (see page 9) are huge areas of sand dunes.

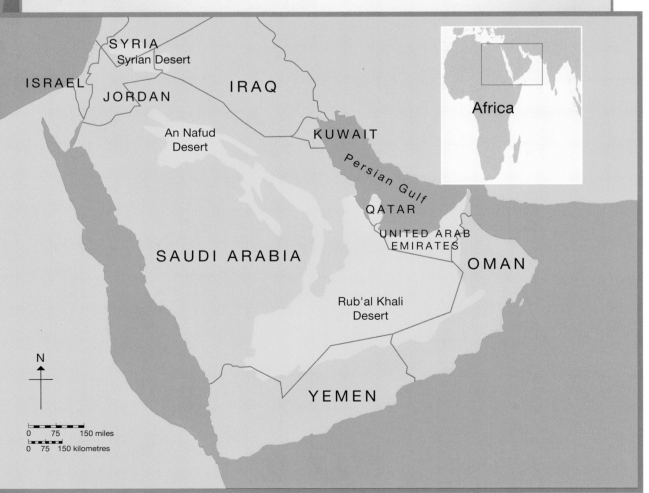

Sand on the move

Like waves on the sea, **sand dunes** are shaped by the wind. They cover up to a quarter of the world's desert areas. Sand dunes move and change shape all the time, as winds blow the sand around. Many dunes form around obstacles, such as a rock, a plant or even a dead animal. The obstacle slows the wind down and makes it drop any sand it is carrying. The strength and direction of the wind, as well as the nature of the obstacle, affect the shape of the dunes (see the different kinds, below). Most dunes are between 5 and 50 metres high, but some are much larger. Seif dunes can be 200 metres high and are often many kilometres long.

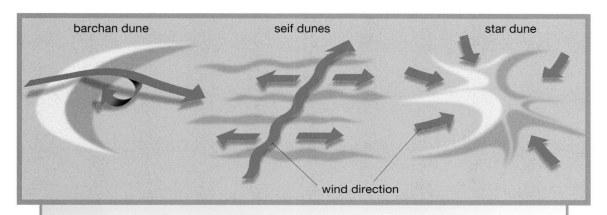

Crescent-shaped barchan dunes often form around a boulder. Their 'horns' point downwind. Seif dunes (from the Arabic for 'sword') are long, parallel ridges. They are often formed when the wind comes from two slightly different directions. Star dunes form when winds blow from different directions. Their arms stretch out from a central peak.

The Empty Quarter

The largest sandy region in the world is in the southern region of the Arabian Peninsula. The Rub'al Khali Desert is mainly in Saudi Arabia, crossing the border into Yemen, Oman and the United Arab Emirates. Rub'al Khali means 'Empty Quarter'. It is called this because the area is so hot and dry that very few people ever go into this wilderness, and there are few animals and plants there. Even though it is 'empty', the region never remains exactly the same. Strong winds constantly blow the sand around, driving it in ripples and waves.

Dawn is breaking over these rocky peaks of the Ahaggar Mountains, in the Algerian Sahara. The highest peak reaches 2918 metres.

Rocky uplands and stony plains

The world's rocky deserts are very hot and dry. Rocky uplands are known as **hamadas**. Some rocky deserts have high peaks. Lower, stony plains are called **regs**. Like **erg**, *hamada* and *reg* both come from Arabic words, and the Arabian Desert has all these different desert types. So too does the world's largest desert, the Sahara.

The Sahara

The Sahara (from an Arabic word for 'desert') stretches over 5000 kilometres (3125 miles) from the Atlantic Ocean to the Red Sea. It covers more than a quarter of the **continent** of Africa and is part of the **landscape** of ten countries. The area of the Sahara is larger than the whole of Australia, and not much smaller than the USA! The Sahara has many **sand dunes**, but they cover only about one-fifth of the desert. Most of the Sahara is made up of *hamadas*. At the Sahara's highest point, in Chad, the Tibesti Mountains rise to 3415 metres.

Death Valley

The **barren** lands of California's Death Valley, in the USA, were given their name in 1849. Many **pioneer** families set out from Utah, looking for a better life – and gold! – in California. Many failed to make it across the hot, bare valley. Among those who survived, one pioneer is supposed to have said: 'Goodbye, Death Valley', and the name stuck. Much of the valley is made up of rock, but sand is also blown into dunes. This is the hottest, driest and lowest place in North America. At one point, near a place called Badwater, the valley is 86 metres below sea level.

⌒ *Death Valley is around 225 kilometres (140 miles) long and 8–24 kilometres (5–15 miles) wide. Many thousands of years ago there was a lake in the valley. All that is left of it now are dry **salt flats**.*

Mesas and buttes

Wind, sand and water all play their part in wearing away land in deserts. This process, called **erosion**, makes many of the common shapes seen in dry **landscapes**. Over thousands and millions of years, rivers can carve out huge **canyons** or gorges, such as the Grand Canyon in Arizona, USA. The canyons divide high **plateaux**, which often wear away further to leave flat-topped, steep-sided areas of highland called **mesas**. When a mesa is further worn away over many years by storms and winds, separate mounds of rock are left. These smaller features are called **buttes**. Mesas and buttes are common in North American desert regions, such as Monument Valley on the Arizona-Utah border.

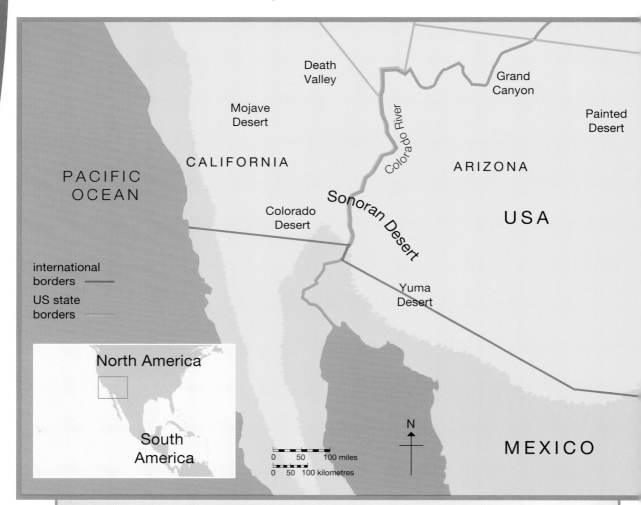

Death Valley

Grand Canyon

Mojave Desert

Painted Desert

Colorado River

CALIFORNIA

ARIZONA

PACIFIC OCEAN

Colorado Desert

Sonoran Desert

USA

international borders ——

US state borders ———

North America

South America

Yuma Desert

N

0   50   100 miles
0   50 100 kilometres

MEXICO

There are many desert regions in the south-western USA. The largest of them, the Sonoran Desert, covers parts of two US states, California and Arizona, as well as parts of northern Mexico.

Rock pinnacles and pedestals

When buttes and single rocks are left standing in the desert, they are gradually worn away even further by the action of fierce winds. The winds carry tiny pieces of stone and sand, which chip and **scour** away at the rocks, like a sandblasting machine, turning them into thin **pinnacles**. Because these winds speed along the ground, the lower parts of tall rocks are worn away more quickly, so they eventually form a mushroom shape. We call these desert rocks **pedestals**.

Sudden floods

Dried-out river beds, called **wadis**, are found in many deserts. They form dry valleys and ravines. Some may have been created many thousands of years ago, when their particular region was not desert because it received much more rain. Today, when rare rain storms do occur, water quickly rushes down the wadis and floods the land. The rushing water carries rocks, stones and sand, which scour the wadis and make them even deeper. The wadi shown below, at the edge of the Sahara Desert in Morocco, has not completely dried out. On flat land, shallow lakes are sometimes left after a heavy storm. These lakes called playas, then dry out in the sun and leave a white layer of salt behind. This happens in Death Valley, California, USA (see page 11).

Changing life

Deserts are harsh places to live in. The plants and animals that manage to survive have to make do with little water and put up with tremendous changes in temperature. Some plant **species** have changed and **adapted** over thousands of years to cope with desert conditions.

Finding and storing water

Desert plants have to find, collect and store the little water that is available to them. Cacti are very good at this. They store water in their fleshy stems. The stems are shaped so that any rain flows directly to their roots. They spread their roots out wide, so that they can gather **moisture** before it sinks far into the ground. Cacti are covered with sharp spines. These protect them from thirsty animals, which would otherwise feast on their store of water.

The giant saguaro (see right) of the Sonoran Desert is the tallest cactus in the world. It can grow to a height of up to 17 metres. Despite its spines, the saguaro is useful to certain birds. Gila woodpeckers peck their way into the thick stem to make their nest. When they leave, tiny elf-owls take their turn in the ready-made hole. The other plant shown here (with many stems) is called an organ-pipe cactus.

Adapting to desert life

Some plants have specially adapted to life in the desert. The *welwitschia* plant of the Namib Desert, in south-west Africa, has adapted so well that it can live for more than a thousand years! It has a huge, 3 metre-long-root and two long leaves. The *welwitschia* takes in moisture from fog and **dew** through millions of **pores** in its leaves, and stores the water in its root. Other desert plants have a very short life. Whenever it rains, they suddenly shoot up and flower within a few weeks. They scatter their seeds before they die. The seeds have a thick coating that protects them through long periods of **drought**. When rain falls, the coating is washed off and the seeds start to sprout.

⌒ *These date palms are growing in the Tunisian Sahara. They can grow up to 30 metres tall.*

Providing food and shelter

Desert plants provide animals with food and shelter. One plant is particularly important to desert people; the **date palm**. In the Sahara and Arabian deserts, date palms grow in **oases** – small areas where there is water. Dates, the fruit of the palm, provide food for people and animals. Date stones can be ground up to make camel food. Palm leaves are used to thatch roofs for huts or to burn as fuel. **Fibres** from dried palm leaves are twisted into ropes. At the same time, the palms provide shade for other plants, such as small fruit trees.

Protection from heat

Most desert animals avoid the fierce daytime heat by sleeping in cool, dark burrows during the day. They are nocturnal animals, coming out to feed only at night. The desert tortoise does this in the dry regions of Mexico and the USA. Some animals, such as the spadefoot toad, bury themselves and go into a long sleep during the hottest and driest parts of the year. This process is called aestivation. When it rains, they quickly wake up and come to the surface again.

Keeping cool

Many reptiles, such as lizards and snakes, are at home in the desert. They are cold-blooded animals and so need heat from the Sun to warm their bodies. They are usually on the move just after sunrise and before sunset, when the desert floor is warm.

The fennec fox, which lives in the deserts of Africa and Arabia, is the world's smallest fox – but it has the biggest ears. This means it never gets too hot, because its large ears help it to lose heat quickly.

Finding water

Desert animals have to survive on very little water. Some insects have **adapted** well to life in the hot desert. Their bodies are covered by tough shells that are coated with wax. The darkling beetle of southern Africa lets **moisture** from morning mist collect on its shiny body. Then it tips itself up to let the water droplets run down to its mouth. Many larger animals manage to survive on the moisture they take in from the blood of their **prey**.

Predators and prey

There are a few large meat-eating animals in the desert. They are **predators** (hunting and eating other animals), and their victims are their prey. The predators include members of the cat family, such as the puma in North America. Dog-family members include the hyena in Africa and Asia and the dingo in Australia. The cats and dogs mainly hunt small rodents, such as kangaroo rats.

The ship of the desert

The camel is well suited to life in the desert. On its back it has a hump (some have two), in which it stores fat. This acts as a food store and allows camels to go for many days without food or even water. Camels can carry loads for long distances and so have become known as the 'ships of the desert'. Camels also provide meat, milk and fleece for desert peoples.

Changing settlements

When early humans spread around the world, they hunted wild animals and gathered roots and berries for food as they went. This was never easy in desert regions, so you might think that people would not want to live there. It is certainly true that fewer people live in deserts than in other parts of the world, but certain peoples **adapted** well to desert life in ancient times. These people did not settle anywhere permanently, but were **nomads** and wandered from place to place to find food.

The Bedouin

Some of the nomadic Bedouin people of Arabia and the Sahara still follow the traditional ways of their ancient **ancestors**. They move around the desert looking for new grazing for their herds of camels, sheep and goats. They often travel at night, when it is cool, and rest during the heat of the day. Families live together in tents made of goat hair.

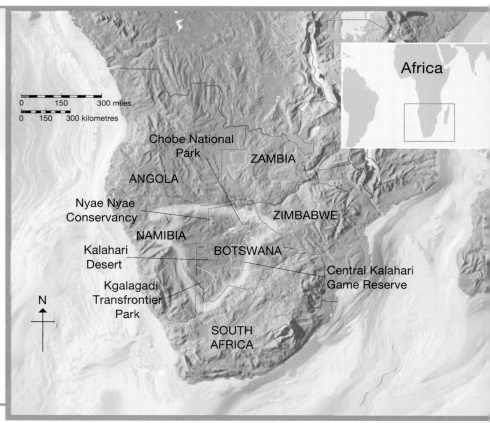

The yellow area, including the Kalahari Desert, shows the region of southern Africa in which the San people live today. This region spreads across different countries and includes several national parks and reserves, where animals and plants are protected.

San Bushmen

The San people, or Bushmen, of the Kalahari Desert are also nomadic **hunter-gatherers**. Their traditional ways have made them expert at desert survival. The men are skilful hunters, using arrows tipped with poison made from special beetles. San women and children spend much of their time gathering roots, fruits and berries. They even get water from the desert by sticking hollow reeds in the dry ground and sucking up underground **moisture**. Their dome-shaped shelters are made from branches thatched with dry grasses. The San people's way of life is changing fast. Once they spread across much of southern Africa, but today there are just a few thousand still living a nomadic life in the desert.

The first Australians

The Aborigines had been living in Australia for tens of thousands of years before settlers arrived from Europe just a few hundred years ago. Over that long period of time, the Aborigines learned how to survive in the dry conditions of their **continent**, which is mostly desert. They hunted kangaroos and other animals with spears and hunting weapons called **boomerangs**, as well as gathering roots and grubs to eat. This traditional way of life was threatened by the European newcomers, but in recent years some parts of the desert have been set aside as protected areas for Aborigines.

Trade routes

In order to be able to cross deserts safely and easily, ancient **merchants** used special routes. They made stops at **oases** on the way, and these developed into settlements. Traders journeyed many hundreds of kilometres to trading posts such as Mecca (which is now a major city). The route was mostly made up of dusty desert tracks, and camels were the best method of transport. Special stopping places for **caravans** of traders, known as caravanserais, grew up along the trade routes.

Takla Makan Desert

The Chinese desert of Takla Makan has a name that means 'go in and you won't come out again'! This shows what ancient people thought of it, but still they travelled around its edges. They followed the Silk Road, an ancient trade route used by merchants to take valuable silk from China to Europe. When the famous Italian explorer Marco Polo travelled that way in the late 13th century, he put up a sign every night that pointed in the direction his expedition was travelling. Next morning, as the desert all around them looked the same, they knew which way to go.

These ruins at the northern edge of the Takla Makan Desert are all that remain of the town of Gaochang. The town was once an important stop on the ancient trade route.

Oasis city

Kashi, at the western edge of the Takla Makan Desert, grew up around an oasis. It became an important stopping place on the Silk Road and was fought over by many different peoples. Today, the region around the oasis city is still desert, but Kashi is **fertile**. Wheat, maize and rice are grown there, as well as melons, grapes and peaches. Today, the city has a population of 170,000.

Phoenix, Arizona

Around AD 1300 Native Americans of the Hohokam culture dug canals next to a river running through the desert. In this way they were able to **irrigate** the land for farming. In 1867 the abandoned canals were found, and a village began to develop. As it grew, the community was named Phoenix, after a legendary bird that rose from the ashes. In 1889 Phoenix, at the north edge of the Sonoran Desert, became the state capital of Arizona. By 1950 it had a population of 100,000, as people moved there to enjoy the warm weather. Phoenix receives just 20 centimetres of rain each year, however, which means that water is in short supply. Today almost a million people live in the desert city of Phoenix (above).

Mineral wealth

Gold, silver, diamonds and other valuable **minerals** are mined beneath the surface of many of the world's hot deserts. Governments often allow companies to develop mines in desert regions, because fewer people live there than elsewhere and so the industry has less of an effect on people's lives. Gold has been mined beneath Australian deserts for about 150 years. Australia is the third biggest producer of gold in the world (after South Africa and the USA), and is rich in many other minerals too.

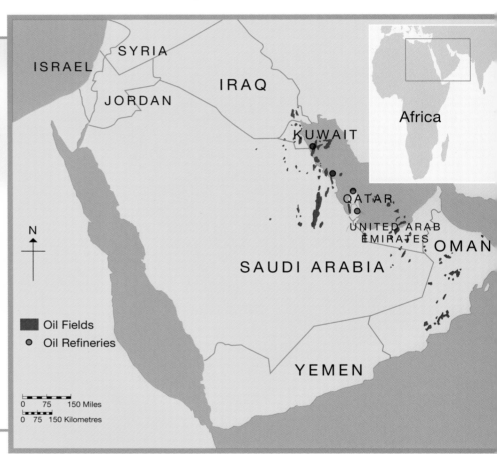

This map shows the major oil fields of the Arabian Peninsula, as well as neighbouring Iraq. The oil is processed at refineries on the coast of the Persian Gulf, before being filled into tankers and sent to all parts of the world.

Namibian treasures

The Namib Desert runs in a long strip along the Atlantic coast of Namibia, in southern Africa. Namibia's greatest treasure is its minerals, and many are obtained from the desert. The main minerals are diamonds, uranium, copper, lead and zinc. These also form the country's greatest **exports**. Many are shipped from the deep-water port of Walvis Bay, which is in a small **fertile** region between two strips of desert.

Oil beneath the sands

During the 20th century oil became one of the most important of the world's natural resources. It is used to power factories and cars and to make plastics and many other products. Oil was discovered beneath the Arabian Desert in the 1930s. The discovery brought wealth and many changes to the countries in the region. The largest of these, Saudi Arabia, is the world's leading producer of crude oil. This 'black gold' is mined in the desert, then pumped through pipelines to the Gulf coast. There it is filled into tankers, which travel around the world. There are also enormous amounts of natural gas beneath the desert.

Solar and wind power

Solar panels can be used to collect the Sun's energy and turn it into electricity. Hot deserts are ideal places to collect solar energy. One of the world's biggest solar-power plants is in the Mojave Desert, California, USA (see below). It generates huge amounts of electricity. **Wind turbines** are also being placed in windy desert regions to generate electricity. This can be an ideal location for wind farms, because in other places local people often say that large turbines ruin the view.

Changing deserts

Many of the world's deserts were formed during the last few thousand years. During this time the world's **climate** has generally changed from cool and wet to more warm and dry – and many deserts are still expanding. The process by which dry regions grow bigger, spread and become deserts is called desertification.

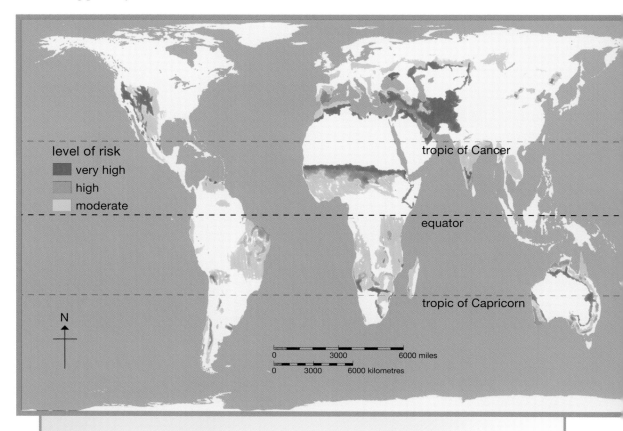

level of risk
- very high
- high
- moderate

tropic of Cancer

equator

tropic of Capricorn

N

0   3000   6000 miles
0   3000   6000 kilometres

This map shows the areas of the world at risk from desertification. The countries of central Africa, at the southern edge of the Sahara Desert, are among those at highest risk.

Climate change

The world's climate is continuing to change, and the overall temperature is still going up slightly. Many scientists believe that this is caused partly by the greenhouse effect, which is created by heat-trapping gases. These allow heat through to Earth from the Sun, but trap it there, like the glass of a greenhouse.

The gases released by burning fuel, such as the exhaust fumes given off by cars, add to this effect. It may cause a general increase in temperature, called global warming. This will make the land drier and add to the problems of desertification.

Increasing numbers

As the world's population increases, there are more people trying to make a living at the edge of desert regions. Many of them graze their animals on land that is already at risk. This is happening in the Sahel, a semi-arid ('half-dry') region that stretches across the south of the Sahara Desert. Cattle and goats are reared there, but a series of terrible **droughts** in the 1970s and 80s turned much of the land into desert. In Niger (one of the countries of the Sahel), it has been estimated that more than a third of the population of 10 million are affected by the spreading desert.

⋂ This herd of goats finds little to eat on dry land near the Kalahari Desert, in southern Africa. Eating the little that is left, herds such as this can turn land into desert.

The Dust Bowl

During the 1930s bad droughts turned a region of the southern Great Plains of the USA into a so-called Dust Bowl. Terrible dust storms forced many people to leave the area around western Oklahoma and northern Texas. The region's soil had become dry and loose after its natural grassland was planted with wheat earlier in the century. The soil simply blew away and left a desert area behind.

Fighting the desert

In the USA, the Soil Conservation Service was set up in 1935 to teach farmers how to protect their soil after the terrible dust storms. One of the main methods was to plant large rows of trees. These help reduce the effect of winds at ground level by getting in their way and breaking up their force. Less powerful winds mean that soil and smaller plants are not blown away.

These people in Mauritania, to the west of the Sahara Desert, are putting up brushwood fences. These help stop sand dunes from spreading.

Controlling rivers

The most obvious way to stop land from becoming desert is to **irrigate** it. In many regions, rivers have been dammed so that people can use water to irrigate their land – but this can bring problems, too. In Egypt, where the River Nile flows through the desert at the edge of the Sahara, the annual flood was essential to their ancient civilization. It spread rich **fertile** mud over farming land. Modern Egyptians wanted more control over the river's waters, and the Aswan High Dam was opened in 1971. This dam stops mud from moving downstream though, so farmers have to use more chemicals to replace the mud's nutrients and fertilize their land.

Tourism

The world's deserts have become popular with tourists. In North Africa, many visitors take camel rides into the edges of the Sahara. Such activities as these bring money to local people, which can help them keep their environment as it is.

Looking to the future

Deserts are interesting features of Earth's **landscape**. As we have seen, they are much more than **barren** wildernesses. Nevertheless, the desert is a difficult environment in which to live. If deserts were to keep on growing, the loss of farmland could lead to **famine** for many of the world's people. As Earth's **climate** changes and if population numbers continue to grow, we will have to make sure that we use land very carefully.

Palm Springs

The popular US resort of Palm Springs, in southern California, lies in a valley of the Colorado Desert. It got its name from the hot springs of the region, but the water from these were not enough to water the desert. This was achieved with water supplied through canals from the nearby Colorado River. Over the last 50 years Palm Springs has developed into a large, desert tourist resort. The photo (right) shows part of the Desert Princess golf course at Palm Springs. It takes a lot of water to keep the course this green.

Desert facts and figures

The world's biggest deserts			
desert	continent	area in sq km	area in sq miles
Sahara	Africa	8,400,000	3,243,300
Australian	Oceania	1,550,000	598,500
Arabian	Asia	1,300,000	501,900
Gobi	Asia	1,040,000	401,500
Kalahari	Africa	520,000	200,800
Takla Makan	Asia	320,000	123,500
Sonoran	North America	310,000	119,700
Namib	Africa	300,000	115,800
Kara Kum	Asia	270,000	104,200
Thar	Asia	260,000	100,400
Somali Desert	Africa	250,000	96,500
Atacama Desert	South America	180,000	69,500

The world's driest inhabited places		
location	country	annual rainfall in mm
Aswan	Egypt	0.5
Luxor	Egypt	0.7
Arica	Chile	1.1
Ica	Peru	2.3
Antofagasta	Chile	4.9
Minya	Egypt	5.1
Asyut	Egypt	5.2
Callao	Peru	12.0
Trujilo	Peru	14.0
Fayyum	Egypt	19.0

This ancient Egyptian temple is on the opposite bank of the River Nile from Luxor. It is one of the world's driest places.

Polar Deserts

The Antarctic ice sheet is the world's biggest polar desert, measuring 12,535,000 square kilometres (4,839,790 square miles). A polar desert is an area where the annual rainfall is less than 250 millimetres, and the average temperature for the warmest month is less than 10 ° Celsius. The Greenland ice sheet is also a polar desert, and measures 1,726,000 square kilometres (666,412 square miles).

> The **continent** of Antarctica, around the South Pole, is the world's biggest ice desert. This is the coldest and windiest place on Earth.

Countries of the Sahara Desert

country	approx. desert area in sq km	approx. desert area in sq miles
Algeria	1,803,000	696,100
Libya	1,462,000	564,500
Sudan	1,179,000	455,200
Niger	1,029,000	397,300
Egypt	878,000	339,000
Mali	755,000	291,500
Chad	604,000	233,200
Mauritania	532,000	205,400
Morocco	82,000	31,660
Tunisia	70,000	27,000

Glossary

adapt to change in order to suit the conditions

ancestor person who lived long ago from whom someone is descended

barren having such poor soil that no plants grow

boomerang curved piece of wood that can be thrown so that it returns to the thrower

butte flat-topped, steep-sided desert hill; a small mesa

canyon deep, steep-sided valley

caravan group of traders travelling together across a desert, usually with animals such as camels

climate weather conditions in a particular area

continent one of the world's seven huge land masses

current strong, steady flow of water in one direction

date palm tall palm tree on which dates grow as fruit

dew tiny drops of water that form on cool surfaces at night

drought long period of very little rainfall

equator imaginary circle that stretches around the middle of Earth

erg area of shifting sand dunes

erosion wearing away (especially rocks)

exports goods that are sent for sale to another country

famine extreme shortage of food, causing widespread hunger

fertile having rich soil and producing good crops

fibre thread-like substance in a plant

hamada raised area of rocky land

hunter-gatherer wandering person who lives by hunting, fishing and collecting wild food such as roots and berries

irrigate to water land, especially using pipes, canals and ditches

landscape natural scenery

latitude imaginary line that stretches around Earth above or below the equator

merchant trader – somebody who buys and sells goods

mesa flat-topped, steep-sided mountain or area of highland in a desert

mineral natural solid substance that is found in Earth's surface

moisture small amount of water; dampness

nomad person who wanders from place to place to find food and grazing land

oasis (plural: oases) area in a desert with water, where plants can grow

pedestal desert rock that has been worn away into a mushroom shape

pinnacle tall, pointed piece of rock

pioneer someone who goes to an unknown place to explore and possibly to settle there

plateau flat area of high land

polar near the North Pole (in the Arctic region) or the South Pole (in Antarctica)

pore tiny opening

precipitation rain, snow, sleet or hail that falls to the ground

predator animal that hunts and kills other animals for food

prey animal that is hunted by another animal for food

rainforest thick forest found in warm tropical areas of heavy rainfall

reg flat stony plain

salt flats area of flat land covered with a layer of salt

sand dune mound or hill of sand formed by the wind

scour to rub hard

species particular kind of animal or plant

tropical to do with the region of the tropics

tropics hottest region of Earth, between two imaginary lines that stretch around Earth; the tropic of Cancer is above the equator, the tropic of Capricorn is below it

wadi dry river valley

wind turbine large windmill that powers generators, producing electricity

Further reading

Discovering Geography: Weather, Rebecca Hunter (Raintree, 2003)

Eyewitness Guides: Desert, Miranda MacQuitty (Dorling Kindersley, 1994)

Mapping Earthforms: Deserts, Catherine Chambers (Heinemann Library, 2000)

The Living Planet: Deserts, Martin Jenkins (Cherrytree Books, 1998)

The Natural World: The Hospitable Desert, Paul Bennett (Ticktock Media, 1999)

Index